a positive approach

Frances James
and Ken Brownsword

D1535750

Playtimes are
happy when...
* the sun shines
* We play with
friends
* people look
after each other

Line drawings by Kathie Barrs

First Published in 1994 by
BELAIR PUBLICATIONS LIMITED
P.O. Box 12, Twickenham, England, TW1 2QL

© 1994 Frances James and Ken Brownsword
Series Editor Robyn Gordon
Designed by Richard Souper
Photography by Kelvin Freeman
Typesetting by Belair
Printed and Bound in Hong Kong by World Print Ltd
ISBN 0 947882 33 2

Acknowledgements

The Authors and Publishers would like to thank Hannah Mary Carpenter and Alfred John Carpenter; Raylene and Natasha Waddington; Shaeron and Kirstine Yapp; Carol McCarthy; Jennifer Cox and children of Southfield Primary School, London, W.4, for their invaluable contributions and support during the preparation of this book.

They would also like to thank P.C. Steve Barrett, Schools Liaison Officer of the Suffolk Constabulary, for assisting in the preparation of the 'Visit to a Police Station' book, shown on page 25.

Caring for Plants in the Classroom - see page 42

Contents

Introduction

It is every teacher's aim to ensure that all children reach their full potential.

This book is about creating a positive, well-ordered learning environment, which values all children as individuals and where all success is celebrated.

Within such an environment children will make optimum progress. They will develop an appreciation, understanding and respect for the rights, needs and feelings of others. They will learn to respect and appreciate their environment and, above all, learn to manage their own behaviour.

We hope that the ideas in this book will help develop such a classroom environment and positive attitudes in our adults of the future.

Frances James and Ken Brownsword

Settling in

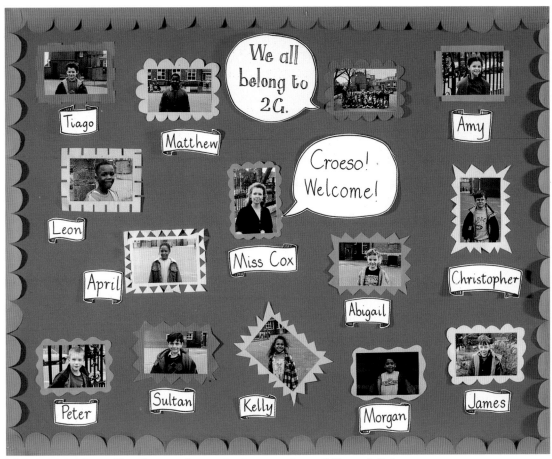

A welcoming display using photographs of the children

When children first start school, or join a new class, it is important that they feel welcomed and that they gain a sense of security as quickly as possible. Creating an atmosphere where the children feel that they belong is a priority. There are many activities which can help to promote this.

When a child begins school for the first time, the school will have a system for obtaining basic information about the children and their families. This may include a pre-admission visit. The information should include:
  - name, date of birth and address, parents' or guardians' names
  - siblings (including the child's position in the family, and the age and sex of siblings)
  - religion
  - dietary requirements/needs

This information will prove a useful focus for initial work with the children.

Photographs. Ask the parents to provide at least two clear photographs of the child. These are used to welcome the child into the class in the following ways:

Coat Pegs. The first thing that the children will probably do on arriving at school is find their coat pegs. Security will be promoted if they can quickly identify their own. Stick one of the photographs by each peg and print the name clearly underneath.

Welcome Display. Attach a photograph of yourself to the display area. Write your name underneath and add a speech bubble containing a suitably welcoming message to the class. (You could include photographs of any other adults who regularly work in the classroom.) Speech bubbles can be added to these photographs - include welcoming messages in other languages, particularly those of the children's families. Attach the photographs of the children with their names clearly printed. Leave space around each photograph so that further information can be added as you engage in further activities. (See photograph on previous page.)

Getting to know everyone!

There are several class or group oral games that may be played to help the children to get to know each other and develop a sense of community. These are of particular relevance for children who have just started school.

All these activities develop the important skills of turn-taking and listening to others.

● Sit the children in a large circle. Start with yourself and say 'Hello, I'm Ms.....'. The child on your right then introduces himself/herself. When the children are beginning to develop a familiarity with each other's names, and to show a degree of confidence, ask them to introduce their neighbours. Relate this to the welcome display (see previous page) so that when children introduce their friends they can then go to the wall display and point out the relevant photographs.
● Play a clapping game with the children. All the group clap twice. Say a child's name. The group then clap twice again and the child whom you named has to say a name of another child. The clapping sequence is repeated and it is the turn of the next child to nominate another.
● With a small group of children, play the 'Who's gone?' game. Sit the children on the floor and ask them to close their eyes. When all their eyes are securely shut, touch one child on the shoulder. This is the signal for that child to leave the area quietly. Once the child has disappeared, ask the remaining children to open their eyes and ask the question 'Who's gone?' Once the missing child has been identified you may use the opportunity to develop the children's powers of observation by asking questions about the child whilst still out of sight. For example, ask about what the child is wearing, the colour of eyes, etc.
● The children can begin to find out more details about their peers by being prompted to ask relevant questions. With the children sitting in a circle, request a child to find out how old another is, how many brothers or sisters that child has, and what he/she likes doing. This exercise develops children's use of the interrogative.

All About Me

Children feel comfortable when talking about themselves and their immediate world, and they welcome the fact that adults are taking an interest in them. This is a reason why one of the first topics for work when children first join a class or school is frequently based on the children. Many ideas for this topic are to be found in *Starting with Me* by Barbara Hume and Annie Sevier (Belair Publications Ltd, 1991).

● Ask the children to draw pictures of themselves and their families. Write the names of the family members on the pictures and add these pictures to the welcome display.

- Devise a simple form about the children. Talk to the children to elicit the relevant answers and then ask them to complete the forms. Some children will need more assistance to complete these. The forms are then added to the display.
- With older children it is possible to extend this activity. Talk to them about when people have to complete forms about themselves - applying for a job, applying for benefits, going to a hospital. Make a collection of different forms to show the children.

'Passports' made by the children

- Discuss passports and identity cards with the class, showing them examples. Talk about the information that would be useful. **Make 'passports' with the children.** Each child makes a small individual book. Cut out a circle and a rectangle from the cover paper so that the paper of the first page is visible. The children draw pictures of themselves in the circles and write their names in the rectangular spaces. The information on the subsequent pages could include height, hair and eye colour, family members, their interests and places of birth.
- Use the information that the children have generated about themselves for a variety of mathematical activities. Gather the children together and ask them to sort themselves into groups using different criteria - all the children with brown eyes, all the children with one sister, etc. This information may then be recorded for display in the classroom. If the children are classifying themselves by eye colour, cut out large eye shapes with the iris the appropriate colour for that particular set. The children draw pictures of themselves which are glued on the relevant iris. If the children were describing where they lived - flat, house, bungalow - cut out shapes of the different dwellings for the children to use. The children glue their pictures on these shapes.

- Use the data to make block graphs with the children.

Display of Work

One way in which children and others are made aware that value is attached to their work is from the care and attention that is devoted to its display. It is important that all children's work is displayed (not just the high achievers or those who produce neat work), that it is changed regularly and that it relates to the on-going work in the class. Clear labelling is necessary to allow the children to see their names - thus showing that their efforts have been recognised, and putting their work into context. Relevant writing around the classroom is also important for developing reading skills.

If the design of the classroom will allow, use the display areas close to specific working areas to display the work produced there. Planning your display areas will enhance the structure of the classroom and so develop in the children the sense that certain parts of the classroom are associated with particular activities. This will help promote appropriate behaviour.

Art Area

Children will be continually producing work from this area which you will wish to display, but it is possible to formalise this by creating a class art gallery.

● Talk to the children about art galleries and illustrate your discussion with pictures from books about different galleries. Talk to the children about the different kinds of exhibitions that can be held - those devoted to one artist, those that have a particular theme or relate to a specific time or period. Explain that some exhibitions are permanent but that others will change quite regularly. Collect catalogues, books or posters from exhibitions. Discuss the famous galleries in the world. If at all possible, arrange a trip to a gallery or exhibition. You will often find that there are small exhibitions in local libraries or theatres.

● Talk about the different types of art that can be found in exhibitions - pictures, sculpture, photographs, needlework, artefacts, etc.

● Plan with the children an exhibition of their art work. Decide upon the theme of the exhibition and what media will be in the show. The children create the exhibits and then talk to the children about how the work will best be displayed. Discuss how different frames are used. Get the children to paint frames for their paintings or drawings. Factors such as visibility and arranging the work so that it is shown to its best advantage need to be considered. The selection of which work is to be shown has to be made. This has to be done sensitively so that everyone feels that his work is valued. One solution is to suggest rotating the work displayed.

● Arrange an opening for the exhibition. Ask the children to make invitations for the 'opening reception'. These could be for other members of staff, other classes, parents or friends. The children make a catalogue to distribute to their visitors.

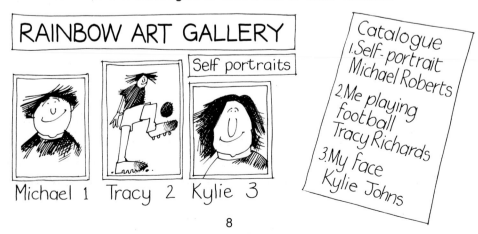

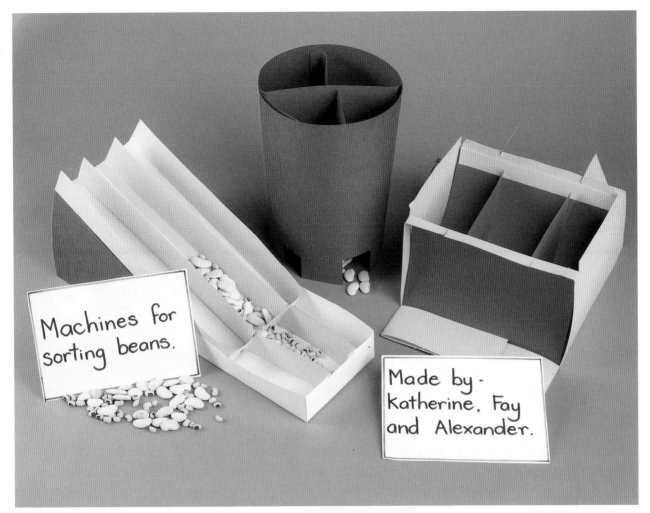

Displaying models to show them to best effect

Maths/Science/Technology

Traditionally, art and language work is the most frequently displayed form of work, but there are many opportunities for displaying work from other curriculum areas. This heightens the importance of these curriculum areas, and further celebrates achievement. When the children have made models they should be displayed in a way that will show them to best effect, but will also protect them from meddling fingers! Label the models. Encourage the children to write about them - how they made them, the purpose for which they have been designed, and how they may be used.

Sand and Water Areas

The children need to be able to explore in these areas, but at the same time there is a need for structure to guide the children towards specific discoveries, and to recognise their achievement. Such a structure will encourage disciplined behaviour.

● Create a 'discovery' board where the children are able to record what they have found through their work and play with sand and water. Establish a theme for discovery - for example, floating and sinking.
Provide a range of appropriate resources and ask the children to investigate which objects float and which sink. Draw a water tank and then ask the children to represent, in a variety of media, the objects that they have investigated and to stick them either on the surface of the water, or on the floor of the tank, depending on what they discovered.

Celebrating Achievement

A positive atmosphere is created in a classroom when children's achievements are recognised and applauded. Academic success is often noted and shared with the children, but social successes and appropriate behaviour is less frequently regarded as worthy of recognition. If these acts or types of behaviour are recorded and praised it will increase the likelihood that they will occur again and will inform the children what is expected of them in the class. This is particularly useful for children who find it more difficult to conform.

● Take every opportunity to praise the children. There is a very useful phrase 'Catch them being good!' When you have caught someone acting appropriately, tell them that you are pleased and the reason for your pleasure. Share this with the other children, either informally or when the class or group is together. Encourage the children to share nice things about each other in class sessions. They are often very happy to report misdemeanours, and it is helpful if you can translate this into reports for the good.

● Formalise these reports by making a display of achievement. This can take many forms. One example is to cut out a large bird shape, possibly a peacock, without the feathers. Get a group of children to decorate the body of the bird with a collage of bright materials, or shiny paper. Attach the bird to a wall. By the side of the bird attach a pouch with blank feathers in. When a child has done something which you wish to praise, write the child's name and their noteworthy act on one of the feathers and attach it to the bird. Involve the children in recording others' good deeds. If a child wishes to report another's good behaviour, his/her name too is written on a feather. (See photograph on facing page.)

● Other ideas for recording achievements include a tree on to which apples of achievement are glued, a flag pole with flags of achievement, a flower bed with flowers of achievement, and a sky with stars of achievement.

● It is important that positive messages are shared with the children's parents, Some parents only ever hear reports of their children's poor behaviour! Make a photocopiable pro-forma which you can use in conjunction with your achievement display to send home to the parents.

● If your school has a good work assembly, ensure that parents are told when their children have shown their work to the rest of the school.

GOOD NEWS! ☺

_____
_____ today
Signed _____

A display recording achievements

● Establish a 'Good News' board in the classroom. Get a child to draw a picture of you and then caption the picture 'I am pleased with these children because......'. When children have done something which you wish to record, ask them to draw pictures of themselves, and to write why you are pleased with them. Attach this to the display. Draw parents' attention to this when they visit the class. Extend this board so that children contribute their good news. Such a display needs to be up-dated very regularly to retain its impact.

● Children writing diaries of what they have been doing in school is another way of establishing good communication between home and school. Talk to the children about how diaries are used in different ways - as aide memoires for what will happen, or for recording what has happened. Keep a large class diary and get the children to record forthcoming events, trips out, class assemblies, visitors. Every day ask a child to check if anything in particular is happening that day. Provide each child with his/her own diary. Establish a routine when the children record what they have done at school in their diaries. Encourage the children to report particular successes or activities which they have enjoyed. The children take these diaries home regularly to share with their families. Explain to the parents the purpose of the diaries and how you hope that they will spend a little time with their children talking about the entries. Develop the idea with the families so that some children might make entries about what has happened at home.

- Discuss with the children about how diaries can be interesting to people in the future, because it tells them what life was like in the past. Tell them about famous diaries such as Samuel Pepys'. Talk about how people might find such diaries. Tell the children how some people have buried time capsules hoping that they will be found in the future. Discuss with the children what they might bury which would give people in the future an idea about their life at school. Cut out capsule shapes and ask the children to draw what they would bury.

Records of Achievement

Many schools are developing Records of Achievement for the children. They are a useful way of creating a sense of achievement in the children, and a vehicle for sharing this with the children's families.

These can take a variety of forms.

- One of the simplest forms is an 'I can.....' book. Make individual books for the children. Stick a piece of paper on the top of the back cover which says 'I can' so that as the pages of the book are turned they are prefaced by this phrase. Talk to the children about all the things that they can do - these activities may be home or school based. The children then record things that they can do on each page and illustrate them. Because of the repetitive format of these books they will reinforce the children's sight vocabulary.

- These books can be supplemented with photographs of the children doing a variety of activities. You may add audio cassettes as evidence of achievement if a child is proud of being able to read a certain book, recite a poem or rhyme, or sing a song. Video may also be used.
- With tasks or concepts that are made up of a series of smaller steps, identify these stages. Construct a checklist so that the children can tick off each element as they successfully complete them. For children who find larger tasks daunting, this technique will make the activity more manageable and will be reinforcing - as they can identify their progress through the task. Also, it improves the children's organisational skills.
- This is an example for making a model castle.

1. Draw the castle you want to make. ☐
2. Choose the boxes that you will need. ☐
3. Get scissors, glue and newspaper. ☐
4. Cover your table with newspaper. ☐
5. Glue the model together. ☐
6. Check if it looks like your drawing. ☐
7. Cover the model with small bits of newspaper ☐
8. Leave to dry. ☐
9. Paint your model ☐
10. Tidy up your table. ☐

● The same principle can be applied to other skills, for example, charting a child's progress in reading. Make sheets or small booklets in which children can record their progress. Include a number of key words which the children will learn as they develop their sight vocabulary. As the children learn them they can tick them off. Write the letters in lower case and upper case to allow the children to record when they have learnt the letter names and sounds.

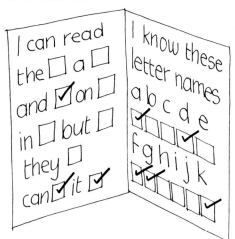

● Present this in different ways. Produce a picture of a clown for each child. When they have learnt the name or sound of a letter they write the letter on a spot which they then glue on the clown's costume.

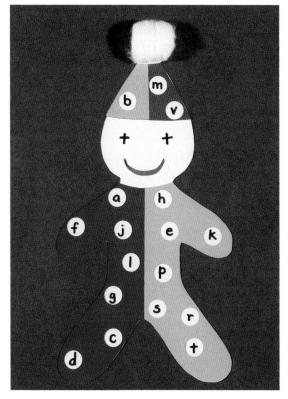

● Use this idea, and similar ones, for the children to record their progress in mathematics - for example, recognising numbers. Some children will find that they need this particular form of support to help them achieve certain social or independence skills: doing up coats, tidying, listening attentively to stories. Allow them to record their achievement in these areas too.

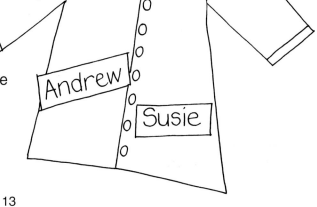

● Draw and cut out a shape of a coat. Let the children who can do up their coats write their names on the coat shape.

Sharing Achievement with Parents

Education is a partnership with parents. Parents are interested in how their children are doing at school. Children like to share their success at school with their parents, and parents also like to feel that they can share in the achievements of their children, and contribute to them. There are many ways of sharing achievements with parents and involving them in your work with the children.

Portfolio of Work

● Each week spend a short time with each child to select two pieces of work that you are both pleased with. Explain to each child why you are pleased, and ask why his/her choice was made.

● Let the child choose one of the two for display on the weekly display wall. The second piece of work should be labelled with name and date of completion and stored in folders designed for this purpose. These folders can be simply made by the children from sugar paper and decorated by them. They can be incorporated into the weekly display. At the end of the week, each child carefully removes his or her work from the display, it is named and dated and then the child places it carefully in his/her folder. At suitable intervals, the children take their folders home for discussion with their parents.

● It is important that the folders build to a range of work completed by the children to show parents the work being covered in your class. A short note from you explaining to the parents why this work was chosen will help parents understand the range of subjects being taught, the range of media being used, and the progress being made.

● These notes can then be used later to form the basis of a summative, termly report of progress. Before starting to send this work home, invite parents into school to see a display of the children's work, and to explain the system.

Display Board of Children's Work

● At the meeting with parents, allow them to spend time looking at the display and folders while enjoying a cup of tea and biscuits.

● Explain to the parents:
  - The work in the folders will be examples of a range of activities carried out during the week.
  - The selection process.
  - Children are not being compared, but the work is the best each individual can produce.
  - THE NEED FOR PRAISE. Let the child do the talking, and praise the efforts made.
  - The need to look after the folders carefully and to return them to school.

Three-dimensional work

Children will complete models etc. which can be included as part of the weekly display, but which they are unable to take home. One way round this is to photograph the work and put the picture in the folder. This can be quite expensive, and thus is prohibitive. A display of three-dimensional work could be laid out once per term and parents invited to visit to see the display, or it could be combined with an official parents' evening. Keep on-going records of children's work.

Recording three-dimensional work

15

Organisation of Classroom

You will wish your classroom to be a purposeful and attractive area, where the children can engage in many meaningful activities. The children will change activities frequently, and you will wish to ensure that this happens in a speedy and efficient manner. Remember an exciting, attractive, meaningful classroom does not have to be a cluttered classroom.

Planning

- Decide which areas you wish to establish within your classroom. Your starting point would be:
  - formal working areas
  - group work area(s)
  - book corner
  - quiet area(s)
  - wet area
  - home corner
  - coat pegs
  - computer area
- Using a large piece of graph paper, draw the outline of your classroom to scale and mark doors, windows, heaters, fixed display boards and fixed furnishings. Mark North on your plan so that you can think which areas gain the most light and at what time of the day. This may affect where you decide to establish your areas. You would not establish, for instance, your book corner in a dark shadowy place in the classrom. Think about Health and Safety. Do not establish your wet area next to electrical heaters or wall sockets, for example.
- Having drawn out your plan of the classroom, cut out the shapes to represent the different areas. Again, make these to scale, thinking about the size of the area you will need, based on the maximum number of children that will use it, seating arrangements, storage, any free standing display boards, etc. It is also very important to consider movement from and to each area. Is there space for children to move without queues forming or brushing into someone else who is busy working in another area? There may be areas of the classroom that naturally lend themselves to certain situations, e.g. coat pegs on the wall by the door, position of sink, fixed book shelves for open display, etc.
- Bearing in mind the above, experiment with your cut-out shapes until you have found what you consider to be the most appropriate design for your classroom.
- Having made your decision, it is important that the plan is displayed in a form that is understood by the children and that an acceptable standard of behaviour is established for each area.

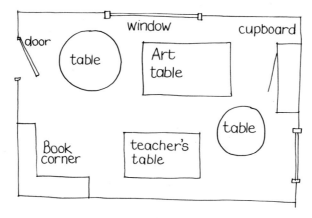

● The plan should be drawn out again, as big as possible within the limits of your display space, and labelled and explained to the children.

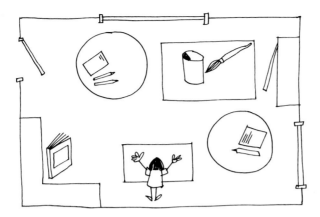

Establishing acceptable behaviour

The classroom should be a busy, lively, exciting place, but it should not be chaotic! You must ensure that you are in control of all situations and that the children fully understand what is expected of them. The children must learn that different behaviour is expected depending upon which area of the classroom they are in. Situational behaviour is a very difficult concept for children to understand, and establishing what is acceptable must be done in a non-threatening collaborative way.

● One of the best methods is to produce 'user friendly' labels for each area which can be explained to the children. The children can help by drawing, cutting out and colouring in the labels. Do not be afraid of asking the children what they think is acceptable. This collaboration can lead to joint ownership of the established protocol. The labels can be displayed alongside each area and/or stuck to the tables.

Collecting equipment/Movement around the classroom

Movement about the classroom and obtaining equipment must be under the control of the teacher. Guidelines clearly understood by the children, and reinforced through display, prevent excess movement and difficulties arising from this.

Availability of equipment

You will have within your classroom a wide range of materials and equipment for use by the children. Some will be freely available, some on request, and some only under supervision. Plan very carefully where within the classroom you intend to store these items of equipment. Store these under the three categories mentioned on the following page.

● Explain carefully to the children what is stored where, and its availability. Set up a system which is simple to understand and which can be illustrated to remind children of the types of access available.

● A very simple, but effective, system is 'traffic lights'. A useful lesson can be constructed around the use of traffic lights and why they are necessary, the three colours being explained thoroughly. Use a model of traffic lights to explain, in particular, the meaning of each colour. A simple model can be made out of cardboard with the three coloured circles glued to the model.

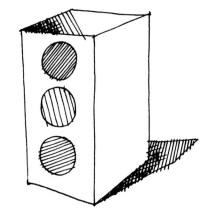

● Having established the principle of green for Go, amber for Caution, and red for Stop, you can explain that you are going to use a similar system in the classroom. Using adhesive circles of three colours, stick the relevant colour on the storage areas as follows:

RED - on all areas where children have no access, for example, storage of dangerous equipment.
AMBER/YELLOW - on all areas where the children must ask your permission before taking any piece of equipment, book, etc.
GREEN - free access as necessary.

red

Lego

amber

green

● Explain carefully to the children what is in each area and why there are restrictions, for example the danger associated with scissors, the need for you to know which book or folder they are using. The children can help with the labelling and the understanding will be reinforced if, following the explanation, they are given white circles and asked to colour them according to the various storage areas. Make a display with the children, illustrating the meaning of traffic lights for your classroom.
● This simple system restricts movement about the classrom, ensures dangerous equipment is under your control, ensures you are aware of what equipment the children are using, and enables lessons to be started and finished in an orderly manner. It also, of course, reinforces the idea that a classroom is an orderly place under the control of the teacher.

Classroom Areas

Formal Areas. There will be times when you wish children to work individually on a given task without discussion with other children. The establishment of a 'formal' area enables children to work quietly without others in the area disturbing them. Without establishing this area it would be necessary for children to attempt to work on their own where others are collaborating.

Group Work Area. This is usually an area where tables are together and children sit around the edge. It is ideal for collaborative work and one must expect a reasonable degree of noise, as the children discuss and share ideas. Ensure that they have adequate equipment to prevent squabbles about who should have the coloured pencils!

Book Corner. Encouraging all children to value and enjoy books is a major aim of all teachers. The book corner enables children to enjoy books of all types. Attempt to have a wide variety of books: fiction, non-fiction, big books, books to look at, read and share. This will become the focus of your classroom. Have books on open display, not all stored on shelves with only the spine showing. Good display of books will encourage the children to explore the written word.

Allow the children to handle and share the books. This is not a quiet area but an area for shared enjoyment.

Quiet Areas. Usually there are two or three chairs and single tables where children may work on their own. This could be for quiet reading, drawing, writing, etc. IT IS NOT A PUNISHMENT AREA. Children sometimes like to get away from the group to concentrate on a piece of work.

Wet Area. One of the most creative and noisy areas of the classroom. This should be set up for wet play, sand and water, art, clay, experimentation, etc. Ensure that the children are appropriately dressed for messy work.

Home Area. Children like to talk about home and their families and much work can be centred on the children's activities out of school. Set up a display area of tables and boards and allow the children to bring in articles from home. This can be developed into a thematic display, concentrating each week on different aspects of life at home. A photographic area can create much interest and provides an excellent opportunity for creative work.

Coat Pegs. As mentioned earlier, much useful work can be focused on the coat peg! It is also important to avoid children pushing to hang up the coats. Establish an order for entering and leaving the classroom, and depositing or collecting their coats. Display children's self-portraits to establish the order for entering and leaving the classroom. Change the order of this display regularly.

Computer Area. When siting your computer, think about the sun on the screen, the trailing flex, etc. Children should not spend too long at the computer, and you should check with the School Medical Officer before allowing any child suffering from epilepsy to use the computer.

Creating Positive Relationships

Children learn very quickly, from experience, their likes and dislikes. These developing attitudes should not be left to chance. It is necessary to assist the children in developing positive attitudes to peers and adults.

We live in an ever-changing world where there are constant demands and decisions to be made. The ability to make considered decisions is a skill that needs to be developed from an early age.

The following are examples of activities which can be provided in the classroom to help the children to develop positive relationships, to make considered decisions, and which are also fun.

People who help me

Children need to learn that there are adults who care for them and will help them in difficulty. The basic list consists of:

Teacher, Welfare Assistant
Nurse
Policeman, Policewoman
Postman
Doctor, Nurse
School Crossing Person
Firefighters
Ambulance Person
Midday Meal Supervisors
Dentist
Lifeguard

Activity One. Collect pictures of all the above. These are usually available commercially. An even better way is to contact your local surgery, fire station, etc. Explain what you are doing and ask if you can take a relevant photograph. You will find that people are very co-operative. For those in uniform it is quite straightforward, but for the others, e.g. doctor, teacher, you will require other prompts to be in the pictures - doctor with a stethoscope, teacher in front of a class.
Having obtained the pictures, fix them to card ready for use and display.

Sit the children in a semi-circle and hand out the picture cards, asking the children to keep them face down on their knees. There may be a number of children without cards.
Ask a child to come to the front of the semi-circle, hold up his/her card and slowly turn so that everyone has seen it. Then ask the group what is on the card - hand up to answer, no calling out, of course! With each correct answer give praise and write the answer on a large piece of paper.

Now collect in all the cards and shuffle them, and hand out to the children who did not previously have a card. Repeat the whole of the activity. This time put a tick by the side of the names on the large sheet of paper. Remember to praise each correct answer. If a child gives

People who help us.

Nurses

Policemen and policewomen

Lollipop people

Children's pictures of people who help us

an incorrect answer, give him/her the opportunity to try again. The importance of the activity is to be able to recognise each professional from the pictures. Children find this activity enjoyable and like the repetition.

Repeat the activity as often as necessary to ensure that all the children have a turn with picture cards.

Activity Two. Have a large piece of paper prepared with the names of the people down the side. A flip chart is very useful for this. If a flip chart is not available, ensure that the paper is displayed prominently and that you can easily write on it. Ask the child with a picture card to come to the front and hold it up for all to see. As a reinforcement, again ask who can name the person in the picture.

Now ask the question 'What does the.........do?'
It is useful to obtain three answers to the question.
List your answers on your large piece of paper by the side of the relevant name. Don't be surprised at some of the answers you get (for example, 'the policewoman locks you up if you are naughty').

Policewoman – looks for lost children
– locks you up

Repeat the process for all the picture cards. This will give you a variety of answers and an insight into some of the preconceived ideas that some of the children have. You are now ready to bring in the idea of 'People who help me'.

Prominently display another large sheet of paper with the same names down the side. Take each name in turn and point at the word and ask 'If you have the picture of a ....please come out to the front and hold it up for all to see'.

Now ask the whole group the question 'What does the..........do that helps us?' Again, obtain three answers for each and list on your paper. Again you will obtain a variety of answers, but this time they will all be positive statements. You can now reiterate to the children that all the people are there to help.

Activity Three. Mount the pictures on your display area with names underneath. Ask the children to draw and colour a picture of one of the people. These can be displayed with the positive helpful statements made previously by the children, attached underneath.

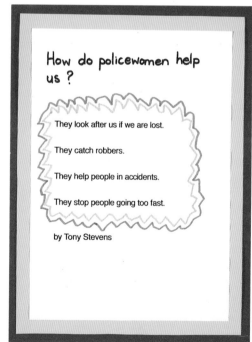

How do policewomen help us ?

They look after us if we are lost.

They catch robbers.

They help people in accidents.

They stop people going too fast.

by Tony Stevens

Activity Four. Give the children examples of situations in which you need help, and ask who would help you.

    If I have a bad toothache I would visit a ....

    If I were lost I would ask a..........

    If I were feeling ill in hospital I would be looked after by a ....

    If I want to cross the road to go to school I would look for a ....

This activity reinforces the idea of helpful people.

Decision-making Skills

We make considered decisions by weighing up the options available, and combining these with past experiences. This historical aspect to decision-making is vital, and one which we must develop within our children if they are not to act purely on instinct. The following activity reinforces the 'people who help me' theme, encourages considered decision-making and introduces the idea of being helped by others.

Activity One.

Sit the children round in a large circle and place the 'people who help me' picture cards face down in random order on the floor in the circle.

Ask each child in turn to find a particular picture - for example 'Sarah, could you find me the Nurse, please?' The child then selects one of the cards and turns it over. If she has the correct card she retains it. If not, it is returned, face down, on the floor.

Repeat the process for four or five different picture cards and then return to the original.

The children will have been watching carefully, and by returning to the original, this gives the next child the opportunity to make a considered choice based on what he/she has observed, rather than at random.

This activity is repeated until all the cards have been selected correctly.

When all the cards have been selected, you can ask the children to say who has a particular card. For example, 'Please put up your hand if you can tell me who is holding the picture of the policeman'.

After practising this activity, it can again be changed to ask what picture a particular child is holding. 'Please put up your hand if you can tell me which picture Malik is holding'.

This adds variety to the activity, keeps the children interested and raises self-esteem, as the children are able to give the correct answers, based on experience.

Another possible change, which challenges the children further, is to use descriptions of events and ask who will help. For example, 'I am feeling very ill and I have pains in my stomach. Who would I go and see?' Having obtained the 'Doctor' answer, you can then ask which child is holding the relevant picture.

Activity Two.

Children particularly like to role play, and this activity can be changed slightly to add further interest. 'Please listen carefully, children. I am going to tell you a story, and if you have the picture of the person that you think can help, please come out to the front and hold it up for all to see. Susan was walking down the street when she saw smoke coming out of the windows of a house.' The child with the picture of the firefighter will come out to the front and show it to the group.

The group should be encouraged to applaud the correct picture. This peer-group praise is very important for the child. Change the pictures around so that all the class have a turn. These activities will reinforce the understanding that there are people who help. They will help to develop considered decision-making, and will ensure adult and peer praise.

Activity Three.
Invite people into the class to talk about their jobs, including members of the school staff. Prepare the children before the guest arrives to think of questions that they would like to ask. You may wish this to be a group activity when the children prepare their questions, and then interview their guest using a tape recorder. The group listen to their recording and decide what important information they gleaned from the interview. Let them decide how they wish to report back to the whole class what they discovered, and how they might wish to make a permanent record of the information. This may be recorded pictorially, written, or by making a further recording summarising their discoveries.

Activity Four.
There are a number of information books about different people's jobs. Support this work by displaying the books in the classroom. You may be able to develop the work further by making appropriate visits with the class, or groups. These may be in school, for example, to the school nurse's office, or the caretaker's room - or outside the school, for example, a visit to the police station. To achieve a focus for these visits, determine a small number of things that the children wish to find out as a result of the visit. Develop with the children a prompt sheet or check list which highlights these points. Ask them to record their discoveries, perhaps in book form.

What time does Mr Clark come to school? ___ How many hours does he work? ___

How many fire engines are at the station? ___

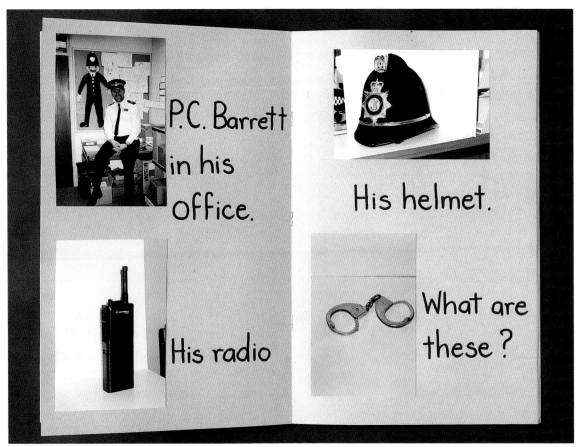

A book recording a visit to a police station, see Activity Four on facing page

Activity Five.
When the children return from their visits, make some 'Did you know?' sheets to display in the classroom.

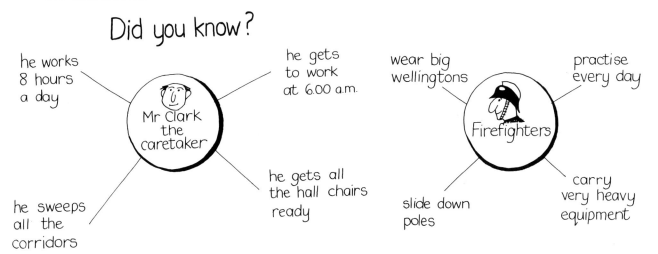

Developing the ability to work in groups
Being able to work as part of a group is a skill that all children must develop from the earliest age.

A variation of Activity One (of People who help me, page 20) combined with decision-making, is very good for developing group work.

The children form a large circle as before, with the picture cards face down on the floor. This time split the children into groups of three, next to each other. Give each group a name.

Children like the names of animals, and thus you could have a dog group, mouse group, etc. Tell each group that they will have to find a particular picture. Explain that they must decide as a group which card they are going to turn over, and whom they are nominating, from their group, to turn it over. All three of the group must put up their hands when the decisions have been made. If their choice is successful they retain the card. If, however, the card is not the one they seek, it is replaced in the same position. Close observation by the other groups should inform their decisions. Teams can be used for all the activities of the previous section.

It is important during these team-building activities that you watch carefully to ensure that no child dominates the others. Use your ability and influence to steer the groups as necessary. Remember there are natural leaders and, at this young age, they tend to dominate. It is very important that the leaders learn to listen to the opinions of others, and that the less forward children have the opportunity to have their say.

For example, 'Jonathan, you have made a number of very good suggestions. I wonder what Lucinda thinks. Lucinda, which card would you choose?'

Please note that you are not criticising Jonathan for dominating. Your comment is positive to Jonathan, whilst giving Lucinda the opportunity to voice an opinion.

Learning to Play by the Rules

By the time many children attend school they will have picked up the fact that there are rules you have to follow at certain times, and to play certain games. They will know that there is a rule about bedtime, brushing teeth, etc. Some will already be conversant with the various board games and sports that they play at home. It is important that children learn the importance of rules as a way of making life easier, rather than something that is imposed by adults on children.

Activity One - Rules we have at home. Start this activity with a brainstorm. Ask the children what rules they have at home, and list them on a blackboard or a large piece of paper. You will be surprised how many you get!

Examples: I must go to bed at 8 o'clock

I must clean my teeth before I go to bed

I must bath every night at 7.30

I can only watch television until 6.30

I must wash up with my big sister on Wednesdays

Having obtained the list of rules, ask the children to draw a picture of themselves obeying one of the rules. Display the pictures on your display area with a relevant caption under each.

A useful piece of mathematics can also be taught using this information. Draw out the axis for a large bar graph on a piece of paper, putting the rules along the horizontal axis and the numbers on the vertical axis. Ask the children, by a show of hands, who has the relevant rule at home. Mark the numbers and complete the bar chart. This can be displayed on your display board.

Activity Two. Having established with the children that there are many rules they have to obey at home, it is important not to leave the activity there. Activity One establishes the information on which to develop the reasons for rules. Prepare a large display paper with the home rules written down (or represented pictorially) on the left hand side, with the child's picture from the previous activity next to the rule.

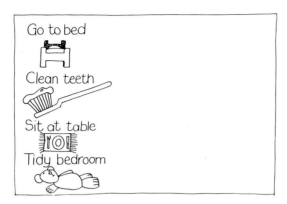

Now point to the first rule (pointing out the picture and praising accordingly). For example, 'This is the rule about brushing our teeth before bed, and this is Manjet's lovely picture. Why do you think we have to brush our teeth before going to bed? Hands up please.'

Listen to and praise the various answers, then summarise. For example 'I think what you are saying is that we brush our teeth before bed to remove any bits of food to stop our teeth from going bad and giving us toothache. Is that right? That's rather a lot to write down, so I will write 'to stop our teeth going bad'. Now ask if the children agree that this is a good rule. You will receive the required answer. Put a smiley face next to the summary.

Continue in this way with all the rules. You will then have listed all the reasons for having rules, and you will have a row of smiley faces.

You may have to use your expertise to steer and prompt the children over one or two of the rules that they will naturally see as not so good - for example, going to bed at 8 p.m. Your prompt may be, for instance, 'If you do not get enough sleep, what will you be like in the morning?'

At the end of this activity you should be able to get the children to agree that:
(a) Rules are important and we should carry them out.
(b) Rules help us by keeping us safe, clean, healthy, and they help us to help others.

While establishing these agreements, give examples - 'Would it be fair to say that rules help to keep us safe? That's right, not playing in the road or in front of cars will make sure that you don't get run over.'

Rules for the Classroom

Having established that rules are necessary, you can explore with the children how you and they can make the classroom a fair and safe place for everybody. Ask them what rules are needed to make this happen. Children usually come up with a very long list and frequently the rules are in the negative. Tell them that you want a fairly short list and that they should be what people should do, and not what they shouldn't. For example, it should be 'Walk in the classroom' - not 'Don't run'. When the children have generated their list, work with them to edit it and to translate the rules into the positive. Have in your mind a priority list of rules that will make the classroom a purposeful and effective learning environment. These priorities might include:

- Ways of gaining adults' attention (possibly hands up)
- Listening to others (taking turns)
- Safety (walking in the classroom and lining up)
- Respect for all (saying positive things about others and being polite)
- Working hard
- Care of the classroom and equipment

Examples of good behaviour. When you and the children are happy with your list, ask groups of children to draw or paint examples of this good behaviour. Write the rules on each of the pictures, and display them in a prominent place in the classroom. (See photograph on facing page.)

Sharing the rules with parents.
It is important to share these rules with others including parents. Get the children to draw smaller pictures of the classroom rules. Make these drawings into a booklet entitled 'Our Rules'. Send a copy of this booklet home to the parents. You may like to give another copy to each of the children to keep. Keep some spare copies that the children can give to visitors to the class.

Once the rules have been established, use them! They will quickly lose their potency if they are ignored. The children will begin to regard them as irrelevant and forget the rationale behind them.

Remind the children of *their* rules at the beginning of each week. If a child forgets a specific rule, for example, runs in the classroom, remind him by saying 'Remember our walking rule' or ask him specifically 'What is our walking rule?' This approach has several advantages. It keeps the exchange brief and positive, and it also reinforces the fact that the child was involved in developing the rules. On some occasions, you may wish to reinforce the reason behind the rule by saying 'We walk in the classroom because it keeps you and the others safe'. Children occasionally think that rules are invented by adults just to restrict children's activities!

Class rules illustrated by the children (see Examples of good behaviour on facing page)

You may develop this theme further by referring to other rules and conventions in society. Talk about rules which other people use, for example, the Highway Code. Ask the children to think of rules connected with motoring, and reasons why they exist. Show the children examples of road signs, either from the Highway Code, or on a short walk close to the school.

Following this activity you may wish to display your classroom rules as road signs:

The rules described above are related to the general classroom environment. If children are having some difficulty in conforming to acceptable standards of behaviour in a particular area of the classroom, for example the play house, develop specific rules for that area.

Ask the children what they think those problems might be, and then if they can think of any rules that might help to sort out the problems. Following the same procedure as with the general classroom rules, keep the list short and positive. Make handouts of the rules which all the children can keep.

This approach is highly effective for individual classrooms, and can also be used for a whole school approach to pupil behaviour, including playground behaviour. It requires commitment from the whole staff, including the ancillary staff. The rules would be negotiated through whole school activities such as assembly.

Rules to Play the Game by

Children need to learn that to enjoy games and interaction with others, there are rules that must be adhered to.

Many of the children will be aware of the need for the rules of games they play at home and sports they go to see or watch on television. In fact, a number of the children will be able to follow quite complicated rules, from games played at home. It is important to realise that it is the reasoning behind the rules that is important.

Games develop the ability to take turns

Games develop positive interactive skills

Games develop self-confidence and a feeling of worth

Games develop a competitive spirit

Games develop the ability to accept losing, having given one's best

Games are of great practical value in developing thinking skills, mathematical skills,
     language and reading skills, and skills of co-operation

Games have value across the whole curriculum

Games are fun!

Activity One. Explain to the children that you are going to make a display of all the games that they enjoy playing. Ask the children to tell you the names of games they play at home. You could end up with a very long list.

List the games on a large sheet of paper and then ask which are the favourite games. This you can do by taking a vote. Explain to the children that you are going to read the list of games to them and that you want them to think about, but not call out, their favourite game. Having read slowly through the list, explain that they can only vote for one game by putting up their hands when you say their favourite. Read the list again, stopping after each game to ask for a show of hands. Put the number of votes by the side of each game.

Now ask the children which game has the largest number of votes. Write this at the bottom of the list. Repeat this to find the second and third most popular games and, again, write these at the bottom of the list. (See photograph on facing page.)

Ask the children to draw you a picture of themselves playing their favourite games. These can then be displayed on the wall.

Ask the children to bring their favourite game (or an artefact from a favourite game, for example, a football shirt) to school to make a display. There are three very important points to remember at this stage:
- obtain permission from parents.
- some games are very expensive and all games should be clearly marked with the name of the child.
- you are using games that develop interactive skills and to widen the children's experience. Many of the modern computerised games are solo activities and should be avoided.

Compose a letter to parents explaining the purpose of your lessons and asking permission for the games to be brought to school.

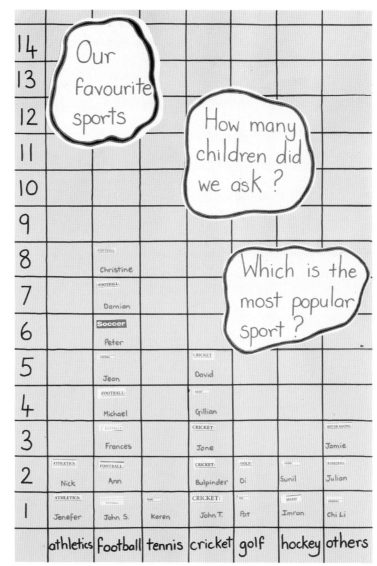

Making a graph of favourite games (see Activity One on facing page)

Dear
We are doing a project on games.
Please may
bring their favourite
game to school. We will
look after it.
Best wishes,

Have your tables ready for the display of games. Display all the games on the tables. You will need a lot of space. Put a stand-up card in front of each game with the name of the child who brought the game into school. (See photograph on page 33.)

Develop the display by asking others to contribute their favourite games. Get the children to ask members of staff in the school what their favourite games are, and if they would bring them to school. Talk to the children about where certain games originated and try to ensure that you have examples of games that are popular in different cultures - for example Ma Jong. Supplement the display with any information books that you can find about games.

Activity Two. You can use the display as a practical aid for mathematics. Questions such as the following can be used:
- Who can count how many games we have on the table?
- How many games are there in boxes?
- Which game is in the largest box?
- Which game is in the smallest box?
- How many games are not in boxes?

Combine this with colour recognition:
- Who can show me a box with red on it?
- Who can show me a box with red and blue on it?
- Who can count how many boxes have red on them?

For children with more advanced literacy skills, ask them to make a list of all the games that you have collected. Introduce the word 'inventory'. Explain that people make an inventory so that they can keep a check on what they have collected. When you dismantle the display, ask the children to check the articles off against their inventory.

Activity Three. Ask for a volunteer who would like to show the rest of the group his/her game and explain how it is played.
You would be wise to start with a game that is not too complicated, for example, Snakes and Ladders. To assist the child, structure the explanation as follows:
'Thank you for showing us your game, Julian. Please tell us what your game is called.' (Don't forget the praise.)
'Snakes and Ladders, Julian. Well, that sounds like a good game. Could you show us inside the box?'

Continue to encourage the child to describe firstly the board (if applicable), the playing pieces and then the rules of the game. Explain to the other children that if they have any questions for the child, to put up their hands and to wait until the child asks them to speak. This helps to raise the child's self-esteem. Once the explanation is over and questions answered, repeat the exercise with another child and another game. You are now ready to set up a games club.

Activity Four. Explain to the children that there are many different games and get them to tell you about what they all have in common - that they all have rules. Emphasise the rules that the children described in their explanations of the games. Children draw or paint pictures of people playing the games, adhering to the rules, and then write one or more rules related to the game underneath.

Talk about the cost of the games and how they are special to the people who brought them to school. From this discussion, draw from the children the importance of looking after the games and putting them back carefully when they have finished playing.

Allow the children to play the games. Select a few, and ask the children to get themselves into appropriate-sized groups. You may ask the child who brought the game in to supervise the first attempts at the game, to check that the others are playing correctly, keeping to the rules and playing fairly.

A display of games brought from home by the children

Once the children have shown that they can undertake this activity sensibly, you can suggest that they run a 'Games Club' during wet playtimes. Establish the general rules of the Games Club with the children. Ask them to explain these to the midday meal supervisors so that everyone is aware of the expectations. The children should understand that the Games Club will be able to continue as long as they keep to the rules. The club can continue after you have removed the display, if you collect together some games for general use in the classroom. Wet playtimes are far less stressful if the children are purposefully occupied.

GAMES CLUB
RULES:
· Play quietly.
· Take turns.
· Share.
· Tidy up carefully.

Activity Five. Provide the children with a collection of magazines and catalogues. Ask them to find pictures of people playing different types of sport. The children cut out the pictures. Bring together all the pictures that the children have found. Ask the children to sort the pictures into different sets. Provide them with a range of criteria - games you play with a ball, games that you play in teams, games that you play in the winter, etc. The children glue the pictures in the appropriate set diagrams.

Games you play with a ball.

Sport you play in (or on) the water.

Activity Six. Get the children to conduct a survey of the sport that members of school staff or members of their families play. This may be approached in two ways. The children go and ask adults what sport they play, or (with your help) the children devise a questionnaire which is delivered to the adults for them to complete. When devising the questionnaire, ask the children to think of all the possible sports that the adults might play. Write these down and put a box by the side of each sport for the adult to indicate whether they play it or not.

When the questionnaires are returned, use the information to construct bar charts of results. Make a book with the children of the sports that the school staff play. The children illustrate the book. (See photograph on facing page.)

SIMPLE GAMES TO PLAY
Explain that games do not have to be expensive, and that it is easy to make one's own games. The children will be enthusiastic about making their own games.

'Knowing the names' game
This game is suitable for groups of six children. Each child draws a self-portrait on a piece of A5 paper with his/her name written underneath. Make three photocopies of each picture giving you twenty-four pictures in all. You will require twenty-four blank pieces of A5 paper, plus one piece of paper with 'Start' written on it, and another with 'Finish' written on it.
Lay the pictures and blank papers in a large semi-circle with 'Start' at one end and 'Finish' at the other. Lay the pictures out in the same order each time.
You will require a large dice and six coloured pieces of card.
Rules:
- Each child chooses a colour and throws the dice. The highest number starts.
- Each child throws the dice and moves around the semi-circle the relevant number of squares, counting the pictures as she goes.
- When the child lands on a picture, she must state the name of the child in the picture. If this is correct she remains on the picture.
- If the name is incorrect, the child is told the correct name and moves back one place.
- If the child lands on her own name and recognises it she has another turn.

This very simple game reinforces:
- the learning of names in the group
- the recognition of the written names
- counting skills
- turn-taking
- co-operation
- forward planning
- language development
- losing 'gracefully'
- the fun in working with others

This simple game can be varied in many ways - all you need is imagination.

The result of a survey among staff members - favourite sports

Talk to the children about how the rules could be adapted. For example, if the child gives the incorrect answer he/she has to return right to the start, OR the number of places thrown on the dice, OR miss a turn. Let them decide which version of rules they wish to play.

To increase the children's involvement with the making of the game, get them to make the dice. Cut out the net of a cube for the children to use as a template. Using light card, get the children to draw around the template and then write the numbers on the face of the dice. Provide some dice for the children to inspect to see the order in which the numbers are written on traditional dice. Ask the children to decorate the numbers and the faces of the dice. Some children may choose to write the numbers, and others may draw the correct number of dots on the faces. Some children may think of alternative ways of indicating the numbers. Hanging the completed dice from the ceiling can create an attractive display.

Making your own dice

As well as developing the personal skills mentioned above, the 'name' game can be used for other areas of the curriculum. Use pictures of animals, different colours or shapes, depending on what you wish to reinforce. You can draw different numbers of objects on paper which the children have to count; or write the appropriate words on the paper to reinforce a specific sight vocabulary.

These games can also be played as hall or yard games by using large pieces of card and a large die. This time the children step out around the semi-circle. This is a very active game of educational value for wet breaks, etc.

Find the .... Game

Children need, on occasion, to let off steam, and activities can be developed that are active learning experiences.

Let us assume the theme is animals. Choose approximately six common animals that you would like the children to recognise by name. It is always useful to display these with names before the game to familiarise the children with them. You will need at least three pictures of each animal.

Sit the children in a semi-circle and divide the children into sub-groups of three or four, e.g. a group of twelve children could be four sub-groups of three, or three sub-groups of four. Assuming three sub-groups of four, give each child a number, counting from one to four. Place the cards face up in the middle, ensuring that there is one card less than the number in each sub-group, e.g. for this example, three cards of each animal.

Explain to the children that you are going to call out the name of an animal and then a number. If it is their number, they move quickly to the centre and pick up the correct picture. The child who does not get a picture sits out of the game. Continue until only one child is left, who is declared the winner.

This game can be adapted in similar ways to the 'Knowing the Names' game.

Simple Card Games

Again it is very easy to create simple card games that can be used across the curriculum as well as developing personal and social skills.

Three of a Kind

You will have seen from the previous games sections that you can decide on the theme you wish to develop and use the games to assist. For this game you will require at least six copies of each card, e.g. if you are using the game to develop the recognition of mathematical shapes you will need to make up six cards with drawings or pictures for each shape.

Rules:
- Each child is dealt three cards face down, and the remainder put face down in the middle of the table. The winner is the first child to have three cards the same.
- In turn, each child may either take a card from the centre pile or ask another child for a particular card.
- When receiving a card the child must say 'Thank you'.
- Any card taken from the middle must be replaced by another card.
- Having received a card from another child, a card must be discarded to the middle pile.
- If the child asked does not have the required card, the turn moves to the next child. If the child has the relevant card, it is passed over and the player has another turn.

MAKING THEIR OWN GAMES

- Following the experience of different kinds of games, develop the work by asking the children to design and invent their own versions of games.

- Bring in to the class a collection of playing cards. Show these to the children. Let them look at the faces. Ask them what they notice about the cards. Turn all the cards face up and ask them to sort them into sets. The children use their own criteria to begin with and so they may sort them by shape, colour, number or by their own criterion.

- Introduce the words - 'hearts, spades, clubs and diamonds'. Draw examples of these shapes and allow the children to decorate them as they wish. Provide them with a range of media - paper, collage material, paints and crayons.

- If you have access to cards from different countries, show these to the children and ask them to describe the differences. For example, Spanish playing cards use different categories.

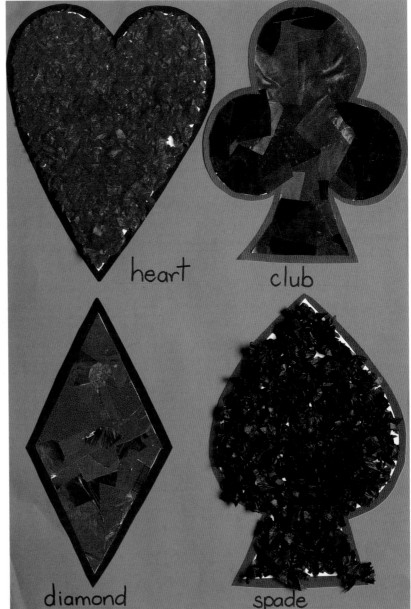

Introducing the card suits

Card designs

- Show the children the backs of a number of packs of cards. Let them observe the designs. Talk about how some cards are used to advertise different products. Cut out some enlarged card shapes and ask the children to design their own card packs.

- Talk to the children about all the games that they have played. Put them into groups of four and ask them to invent a game of their own. Provide them with a range of materials - card, glue, paint, felt-tip pens etc., which they may need. Tell them that they should discuss amongst themselves the type of game that they wish to make. Do not allow them to start to make the game until the group has been to tell you what their plans are. As they are discussing, try to listen into the different groups and encourage the more reticent members of the groups to make a contribution. Praise the less vocal children for any suggestions that they make and the more assertive children for listening to their friends.

- Once the children have made the game, let them play it to see if they have to make adaptations to the rules. Once they are satisfied with their games, draw the children together and ask each group to explain to the others their own game. Encourage each member of a group to make a contribution.

- Organise a session when the children have the opportunity to play each other's games. At the end of this session ask them to tell you what they thought of the game. Explain to the children that everybody worked very hard on the games, and so what they say must be positive and any suggestions must be to make the game *even better!*

- Display the games carefully. The children, or an adult, can write out the rules of their game to display by the side. The children can also make and decorate boxes or folders in which to keep the games safely.

Playground Games

A classroom frieze of a happy, active playground - made to consolidate work on playtimes

Many of the behavioural problems that arise in the playground occur because there are insufficient activities for the children. Playground areas can be bleak places which do not encourage productive and positive play. Looking at the playground environment to see how the space can be used to best advantage is a profitable exercise. As a whole staff, explore ways of creating areas for different activities - quiet areas where children who do not wish to run around can be, and areas where more active games can be played. Involving children in these discussions is important. Their involvement will mean that they will be far more likely to adhere to any rules associated with the areas and that they will care more for the environment.

Get the children to think what makes a 'good' playtime for them and when it is not good. Write a list with the children of all the factors that contribute to a happy playtime. This might include good weather, having a friend to play with, children sharing and looking after each other. Ask a group of children to illustrate this list.

39

This list may be recorded by words or pictures. As the children will be sharing playtimes with the children from other classes, this technique is even more powerful if they can share their ideas with children in the rest of the school. This could be through an assembly or by making presentations to other classes for the other children to discuss. They will also realise that their suggestions are taken seriously if they are able to explain them to the Headteacher. If some of their suggestions are taken on, ensure that all the staff involved at breaktimes, including the midday meal supervisors, are informed of what the children are hoping to achieve. The children can share the information by making small publicity handouts of their good ideas.

Traditional playground games

After the children have spoken about games that they play, you can introduce them to other games that they may not know. There is a wealth of traditional playground rhymes and games and these have been collected in a number of books. Share these books with the children. Ask the children to ask members of their families about the games that they used to play when they were at school. If some of these games involve rhymes, ask the parents to write them down or to record them. Identify the games and rhymes that the children express most interest in and teach them to the children. This may be in P.E. lessons or when you are on playground duty. Explain what you are doing to other supervisory staff and ask them to encourage, and play with, the children. Make a book with the children of all the playground action rhymes that they have collected. Record or video the children saying some of the rhymes. Make other books of children's games. Use photographs of the children playing successfully to illustrate the book. (Children are always fascinated by photographs of themselves.)

Importance of routine

The beginning and end of playtimes set the tone for the following session. If the children have a calm and established routine at either side of the playtime, it will influence their approach to what follows.

Dinner Times

Eating together is a social time and, at its best, is a time when people share and converse. In schools it can be a fraught time due to the pressure of delivering a large number of meals to the children in environments which are not best suited for the purpose. Despite these limitations, there are things which you can do to improve the quality of the experience. As a whole staff, look critically at the present arrangements for dinner times and see how they can be improved. Is the environment as attractive as possible? Are all members of staff, and the children involved, conscious of the standards of behaviour that you are trying to promote? Are the ways that children enter and leave the dining area as streamlined as possible? Are the children praised for positive behaviour at dinner times? Do the children have opportunities for responsibility at this time?

Clock faces
Draw some clock faces. Ask the children to draw in the time that they eat different meals. Provide the children with paper plates. Let them think of their favourite foods for the different meals, and then draw the food on the paper plates. Stick the clocks next to the relevant plates. The display can be developed further by the children thinking of whom they like to eat with.

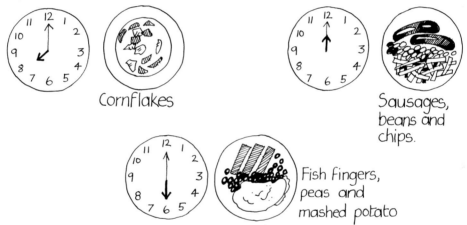

Cornflakes

Sausages, beans and chips.

Fish fingers, peas and mashed potato

A class meal
Plan a class meal which will be prepared, served and eaten by the children. Decide, with the children, what the menu will be. You will have to influence the decision if the menu becomes too complex. A shopping list is prepared and a group of children could be involved in going to buy the ingredients. Involve all the children in preparing the meal and setting the tables. Talk to the children about who is going to serve elements of the courses. Discuss the kind of behaviour that they will expect from their peers - waiting for everyone to have been served before starting, using the words 'Please' and 'Thank you', making sure that everyone has all that they require. During the meal, quietly highlight children who are demonstrating such behaviour. The children may wish to ask a special guest to their meal.

Liaison with supervisors
Talk to the midday meal supervisor who has the responsibility for your class. Tell them that you wish to have a daily report of children who have behaved particularly well. It is important that it is not always the same children who are mentioned. Encourage the supervisors to 'catch' a wide range of children being good. Share this with the children and praise the children who are the subjects of these reports. Be explicit about the behaviour you are praising so that the children can learn what pleases you.

Caring for Living Things

Developing caring attitudes can extend to other living things, not just people.

Plants in the classroom

Set up an experiment for the children to discover what plants need in order to thrive. Bring a packet of seeds into the class. Mustard and cress seeds are particularly suitable as they grow quickly and the children can see the results in a relatively short time. Show the seeds to the children. Ask them what they think the seeds will need in order to grow. The children will come up with a variety of suggestions. Take a note of these. Explain to the children that you are going to experiment to find out what is necessary to grow the plants. Using the children's suggestions, allow the children to create different growing environments. (You may need to steer the ideas to get a full range of possibilities.) Decide with the children if you want the seeds in soil or sprinkled on blotting paper.

The possible variations include:
- one pot/tray watered and in the light - plus given plant food.
- one pot/tray watered and in the light, but not fed with plant food.
- one pot/tray with neither water, light nor food.

Ask the children to make labels describing the conditions.

Every day ask the children to observe the progress of the seeds. Make a book to record the observations. Assign a page for each condition. Children record their observations every day. When one of the pots has successfully grown, collect all the other pots and discuss with the children what has happened. Encourage detailed observations, the children measuring the height of all the plants and noting if the stalks have grown straight or have leant towards the light. The children could also taste the cress to see if they can detect the difference!

From the observations, encourage the children to think about the conditions necessary for plants to grow successfully. Make a display entitled 'How we care for plants', and get the children to make posters of the key features of plant care.

Looking at seeds

Develop your plant area by discussing the different kinds of seeds that you can grow. Bring a collection of fruit to school. These may be edible fruit, or fruit from trees or plants. It is very important that the distinction is made clear to the children and that they do not try to eat inedible fruit. Cut the fruit open and ask the children to identify the seeds. Tell the children that you are going to try and see which ones will grow. The children plant the

Caring for pets - see page 44

seeds and label the pots, identifying the type of seed. These labels can be attractively decorated. Each child has the responsibility for caring for their seed. Reinforce the type of thing that they will have to do to look after their plants. Praise the children when you see them taking care of their seeds.

Bring in a collection of seed packets and show the children the instructions on the back of the packet, describing how you plant the seeds and the subsequent care that is needed.

A school garden

If there is a suitable area of soil in the school grounds, develop the activity by planting flowers and vegetables. Discuss with the children the different aspects of care for plants outside - why it is not necessary to water them unless there is a particularly dry season, but why it will be necessary to weed around the plants.

Get the children to draw pictures of the plot of land at different times of the year. Keep these pictures to enable them to begin to appreciate the passage of the seasons.

January   April   July   October

Pets

Many of the children will have the experience of looking after pets, or observing others taking care of pets, at home.

Discussion

Talk to the children about pets, and about the kinds of pets that people keep. Ask them if they have pets at home. Structure the sessions so that children have the opportunity to question individual children about their pets. This activity develops listening skills and self-confidence. You may have to prompt them by suggesting suitable questions.

Caring for pets

Develop the activity by getting the children to tell you how they take care of the pets, what the pets need - for example water, food, exercise, grooming, cleaning of cages, etc. Try to elicit from the children the reasons why the animals need such attention.

Arrange the children in groups. Let them choose one type of pet and then one or two children paint a picture of the animal. Others in the group paint pictures of things that the pets need - water bowl, clean cage, etc. Cut out large arrows and display the children's pictures with the arrows linking the animal with the appropriate requisites.

Draw up a table with a number of different pets along the top and the forms of care down the side. Ask the children to look at the display and then tick the correct box if that pet needs that form of care (see page 43).

From this information, some children will be able to work out how many of the pets that they have chosen require exercise, food, etc. They will discover that there are certain things that all pets need and other things that only specific animals require. Ask them why they think this is.

Focus on one specific aspect of care, for example, food. Ask the children to discover exactly what kind of food their pets eat, how much food the pet eats, and how often the animals have to be fed. The children report their findings to the whole group.

Caring for the School Environment

Developing in the children a sense of responsibility for the school environment is important. With such an appreciation it is more likely that the children will endeavour to take care of the fabric and equipment of the school.

People responsible for caring for the school.

Talk to the children about who looks after the school. In this discussion they will probably identify the caretaker and the cleaners. Introduce them to the idea that everyone who is in the school has a responsibility for looking after it.

Arrange with the caretaker for the children to visit his room. The purpose of this visit is for the children to see what kind of equipment is needed to care for the building and to develop an appreciation of the work involved.

On the return to the classsrom, get the children to make a picture of the caretaker and the pieces of equipment, tools, etc. that they found. Display the picture with captions under each utensil, describing its use.

Posters advertising a recycling scheme

Talk with the children about ways that all the school community can help the caretaker and the cleaners in their work. Display the children's suggestions.

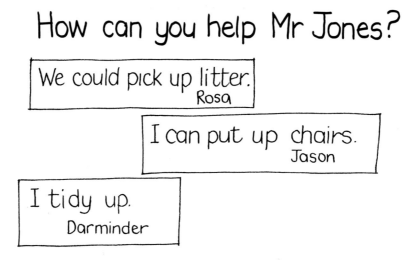

The problem of litter

Litter is often a problem! One of the ways of addressing this is by having a rota of children who are responsible for picking it up, but it is preferable that all the children share the responsibility.

Talk to the children about the types of litter bins that you can see. Try and bring in pictures of unusual ones. In China the litter bins are frequently large ceramic frogs, and people feed the litter into the frog's large open mouth. Draw from the children the fact that the litter bins are designed so that the litter doesn't blow out again. Set the children the task of designing a litter bin. Ask them to make it as attractive as possible, to encourage people to use it, but also one that is practical. Display the children's designs. Allow the children to make models from their designs.

Posters - recycling materials

Talk to the children about how things can be recycled. If you have the space in the school and a suitable outlet, start a collection of things that can be recycled. The children may wish to bring articles from home to add to the collection. Get the children to make posters advertising the scheme (see photograph above). Add any litter that the children find around the school premises to the collection.

Caring for the Home Environment

The work that the children have been undertaking about the school environment can be extended to discussion on the care of homes. Housework is an undervalued activity, but through careful exploration its importance can be highlighted. When discussing the topic with the children, ensure that housework is not seen as the preserve of one gender!

Work in the house

Open the discussion by asking the children to describe all the activities that have to be done in a house. Fold large pieces of paper in half. Cut the top third into the shape of a roof. Divide the inner piece of paper into four equal rectangles. These are four rooms of the house - the sitting room, the kitchen, a bedroom and the bathroom. Talk with the children about the kind of furniture you find in each of the rooms. Ask the chidlren to draw an exterior view of a house on the outside fold of paper and to illustrate the rooms with relevant furniture. When they have completed this, ask them to think about types of work that are particular to those rooms - for example, making beds in the bedroom, washing-up in the kitchen, etc. Get them to write the tasks in the appropriate rooms.

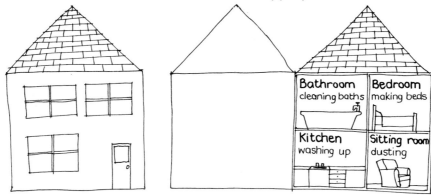

Talk to the children about what jobs they do around the house to help. Ask the children to draw pictures of themselves. Cut out speech bubble shapes. The children write in the speech bubbles describing what they do to help.

The home corner

This work can be extended through the children's play in the home corner. Discuss with the children how they look after and tidy the home corner. Provide the children with suitable equipment to permit them to carry out the tasks.

If the children are involved in cooking at school, make sure that they are involved in all aspects of the exercise. This includes the washing up, tidying away, sweeping up and cleaning any surfaces.

Exploration of Feelings

Exploration of a range of emotions will make children more aware of their feelings and, possibly, ways of controlling them.

Begin the work by asking them to think of all the feelings that they can identify. Make a list with the children of all their suggestions. Talk about how some words can be used to describe the same feeling. Identify any synonyms that the children have proposed.

happy = cheerful = glad

(You can extend this work by talking about other synonyms.)

Discuss with the children the feelings that they enjoy and those that they might find uncomfortable. Cut up the list of feelings and ask the children to sort them into the two appropriate sets.

We like feeling

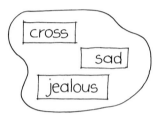

We don't like feeling

Discover from the children what things can trigger a range of emotions in them - what makes them happy, sad, angry, jealous, etc. Make small books for the children. Ask them to complete the phrase 'I feel...when...' on every page, and to illustrate their statement with a picture.

When the children have completed their books, ask them to read them to the other children. Explore the differences and similarities between the children's reasons for specific emotions. Choose one emotion - it is better to choose a positive feeling - and ask the children to paint a more detailed picture of what makes them feel that way. Display these paintings.

I feel happy when people play with me.

I feel happy when I walk my dog.

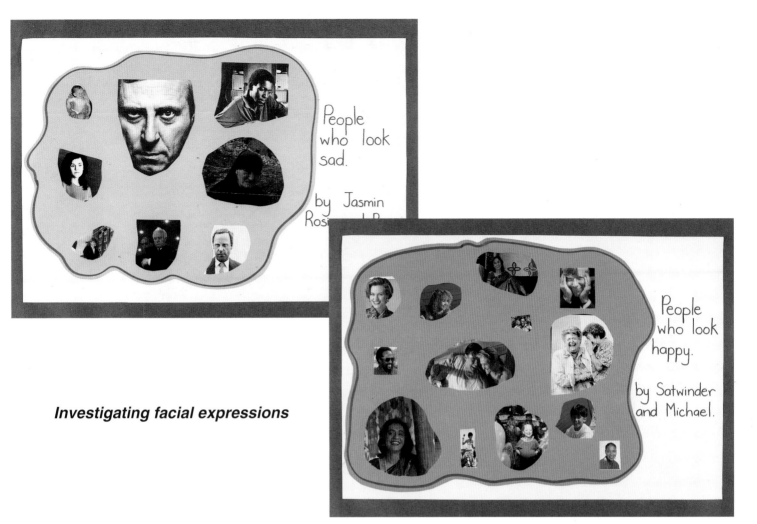

Investigating facial expressions

Talk with the children about how people's facial expressions change when they are experiencing different emotions. Gather together a collection of magazines and ask the children to find photographic examples of people displaying different emotions. The children then stick the photographs on to suitably labelled pieces of paper.

It is important to develop in the children an empathy for how others are feeling. The exploration of different facial expressions (see photograph above), is a way of beginning this work. Ask individual children to pretend that they feel a certain emotion. As the child holds the pose, ask the others what they notice about the child's body posture, etc. Draw from the children other things that people might do if they were in a particular emotional state - for example, a happy person might whistle, sing, laugh, etc.

If the children have an awareness of how others feel, this in turn may have an effect on their own emotions. For example, if someone is feeling angry the other person might feel frightened or angry themselves. This should be explored with the children.

Talk to the children about what they do and feel when they recognise another person or child is feeling sad or happy. Through the discussion it will probably become apparent that the positive emotions are often 'catching', and if someone is feeling happy that may well make others feel happy too. Other emotions are more complex. Explore the range of options available to the children if they encounter an angry person: walking away or ignoring them, until they feel happier, may be the most appropriate response.

The children should reach the conclusion that it is preferable for people and their peers to feel happy. Focus the discussion on things that they can do which are likely to make others feel good and how they can demonstrate that they care about others. Brainstorm with the children all the ideas that they might have to achieve this.

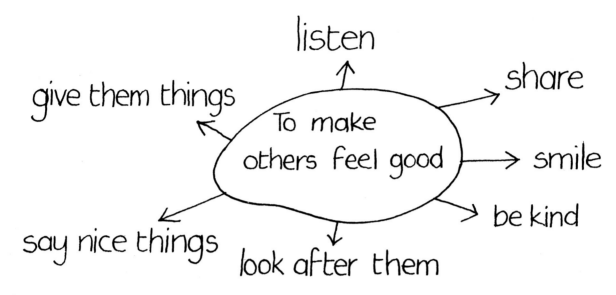

Ask the children to report any incident when one of their peers did something that made them feel happy or cared for. Share these incidents with the rest of the class, praising both parties, the children who reported the occurrence and the child who did the good deed. Record the names on a prominent board. It is important that this is kept up to date.

This work can be supported by role play and drama. There are also a number of relevant songs that you may wish to teach the children - 'I'm H-A-P-P-Y', 'Poor Jenny lies-a-weeping', 'If you're happy and you know it'.

Stories as inspiration

Sorting the characters into sets according to characteristics (see below)

Stories are a very effective way of developing children's appreciation of acceptable behaviour, the ways in which people's behaviour affects others, and how people have choices about their behaviour.

Many traditional stories have a strong moral element - good and evil strongly portrayed in the characters. This facet can be exploited to help children recognise desirable personality traits and to postulate why people might act in a certain way.

Characterisation

Tell the story of 'Cinderella' to the children. Ask the children to name all the major characters in the story and then to draw the characters. Cut out the children's drawings. Hold up the pictures and ask the children to say whether they feel that the character is kind or unkind. Sort the characters into two sets according to the children's classification. The children stick the pictures in the relevant set. Show the sets to the children and get them to justify their decisions - for example, 'Cinderella's father is unkind because he lets the sisters boss Cinderella around'. The children may find it difficult to justify some of the decisions. This is an interesting discovery for the children and may result in their deciding that they do not have sufficient evidence to support their classification. (See photograph above.)

Develop this activity by asking the children why they think the characters are as they are. They may suggest, for example, that the sisters are unkind to Cinderella because they are jealous of her looks.

Some 'heroes/heroines' in traditional stories are not uniformally 'good', and this should be drawn to the children's attention. Ask the children what they think of Goldilock's going into the three bears' house, or Jack (of beanstalk fame) stealing the giant's gold or hen.

In certain stories the characters display different attributes at different stages of the story. Tell the story of 'Hansel and Gretel' to illustrate this. Once you have related the story, go through it again with the children, ensuring that they have the sequence of the story firmly established. Divide the children into groups to illustrate the story. (The story lends itself to collage work.) Display the story sequence on the wall with a caption describing the children's pictures. Leave a space under each picture. Focus on the character of Hansel with the children. Talk to them about what they think of Hansel and how he might be feeling at each point of the story. The children should note characteristics such as bravery and foolishness in the same character. Get the children to write short commentaries about Hansel at the different points of the story. You may wish the children to illustrate the commentaries. Display these under the relevant picture.

Ensure that in your repertoire of stories you include ones that relate to people and children who are different from themselves. Stories introduce children to the wider world. The discussion which follows the story promotes an understanding and appreciation of the diversity and richness in the world. The romance of stories is an important feature, but take care that not all the stories you tell romanticise or distort other cultures, religions or groups of people. Whenever possible, support the stories by showing the children artefacts or pictures which relate to the theme of the story.

Making decisions

There are frequently points in stories when the characters have certain choices to make. The choices that they make influence the subsequent course of the events. This reflects life, where we are constantly faced with choices and we need to make informed decisions about the best options for ourselves and others.

Thinking of alternatives

Choose stories in which characters have to make certain decisions, and discuss with the children what they would have done and why they would have made those decisions. Begin with stories where characters have made obviously sensible or silly decisions. A good example is 'The Three Little Pigs'. Retell the story with the children. Make small concertina books, with six pages. Draw a line dividing each of the pages in half horizontally. Ask the children to draw a picture of what each little pig chose to build his house with, and what happened when the wolf came along to the house. These pictures are drawn on the top half of the pages. Bring the children together and talk about what else the pigs could have made their houses from, and how that would have affected the outcome of the story. The children then draw an alternative version of the story on the bottom half of their books.

Develop this idea of 'if.........then.........would have happened', using a range of well-known stories. Propose a number of alternatives to the children and collect their suggestions.
Examples could include:

'If the gingerbread boy had stayed with his family..........'
'If Jack had sold the cow for money, and not for beans..........'
'If Red Riding Hood's grandmother had not opened the door to the wolf..........'
'If Sleeping Beauty's parents had asked the thirteenth fairy to the christening..........'
'If the dwarves had not invited Snow White to stay with them..........'
'If the boy had not cried 'Wolf'..........'

Let the children choose one of these examples and illustrate the revised condition and result with two pictures. Cut out some brightly coloured arrows and display the new story equations (see photograph above).

If the dwarves said "Go away"

then Snow White would be sad.

Thinking of alternative developments

Stories to reinforce a theme

Certain stories can be used to reinforce particular themes or topics which are current in the class. For example, the theme of helping people is the central one in 'The Little Red Hen'. In the story, the little red hen asks all the other animals if they will help her at various stages of the bread-making process. At each stage all the animals decline to help until it comes to eating the bread, when they all volunteer to help! Unsurprisingly, the little red hen decides to eat the bread herself.

The story has an attractive repetitive structure which will encourage the children to join in as you tell it. Get the children to paint pictures of all the characters at a specific episode of the story. Cut out speech bubbles and get the children to write in the responses from all the animals.

Talk to the children about the little red hen's reaction, and whether they consider that it is fair.

Extension activity - making bread

If it is possible, bring to the class some ears of wheat. Using a pestle and mortar, let the children grind the wheat to see how flour is made. Talk about different kinds of mills that are used to grind corn - the old-fashioned ways using wind and water mills, and the modern flour mills.

Bring in examples of different kinds of flour for the children to look at.

Make bread with the children, involving them at all stages of the process. When the bread has been made, remind the children of the sequence of the bread-making process. Record this and display on the wall. Enjoy eating the bread with all the children.

Read the children other stories about people helping others. Let them develop their own stories. This can be an individual activity or one that is undertaken by small groups of children, which they then retell to the rest of the class.

Use fables and cautionary tales to emphasise certain teaching points. A word of caution - some cautionary tales are quite violent and may not reinforce the behaviour that you desire!

Drama and role play

Drama and role play are ways of exploring children's reactions and emotions in different situations.

Drama sessions need to be tightly structured and well-planned or they can be a source of ill-discipline or situations where a few children dominate the proceedings. Establish a few ground rules at the beginning of the session to reduce the likelihood of this happening. These rules should include taking turns and listening to others.

Investigating reactions through drama

Plan some situations that illustrate a particular aspect of behaviour.

Children's responses to imagined situations

For example, you might wish to explore with the children what they could do if they felt that someone had taken something that belonged to them. Describe the initial scenario to the children - they have lost their favourite model dinosaur. When they are in the playground they see an older child playing with a dinosaur which looks just like theirs. Allow the children to work in groups to decide what they would do in such a situation. Each group enacts their solution. When each group has performed their piece, bring the whole class together to discuss what they have seen and the merits, or otherwise, of the proposed solutions.

Slightly adapting the situations develops this activity. Would the children's responses be different if the lost object was their mother's watch, or if the person seen with the object was a younger, smaller child, or an adult? Propose alterations to the children and let them revise their responses.

After the drama session, repeat the scenario to the children and ask them to write down, individually, what they would do. Write the prompt on the top of a large piece of paper and stick the children's responses on to the paper. Some children may choose to word-process their responses (see photograph above).

Teach the children how to 'freeze' when in the middle of their dramatic representation. Ask the other children what possible actions could be taken at that point of the story and then instruct the 'actors' to continue, following the advice of the rest of the children.

Use drama to enact well-known stories, described in the previous section, to develop the idea of positive behaviour.

Puppets

Puppets are an extension of the drama activities. Their slightly more abstract qualities allow you to explore more controversial or confrontational aspects of behaviour. Use either commercially-produced puppets or ones that the children have made for themselves.

To make hand puppets

Cut out a simple template shape. (Make sure that the base of the puppet is wide enough for the children to put their hands in.) The children draw twice round the template on felt, and then sew around the edge of the shapes, using back-stitch if they are able to. They add certain features to the basic shape to personalise their puppet: ears, etc. for animals; hair, facial features for people.

To make stick puppets

Children draw, using felt-tip pens, the characters for their puppets and then cut them out. Stick the drawings on to some card to strengthen them. Use strips of balsa wood to stick to the puppets. The wood can be stuck either horizontally or vertically to the puppets.

If you are using stick puppets, create a puppet theatre for the action. Use large cardboard boxes. Cut out a large rectangle at the front of the theatre and slots in the sides of the theatre to allow the puppets to be slid in and out. Cover the box with white paper and allow the children to decorate the front of the theatre. Show the children pictures of old-fashioned puppet theatres, emphasising the rich decoration. Provide the children with suitable materials, sequins etc. to recreate a similar effect.

Exploring situations

Determine a number of scenarios for the puppets. They are particularly useful for exploring situations in which violence is used to attempt a resolution. For example, one of the puppets might be a 'naughty' cat who is always tripping up other animals. The other animals have a meeting to decide what they can do about the cat. You will probably find that the other animals decide that they are going to teach the cat a lesson, which could be tripping her up or

The animals hit the cat.

The animals play with the cat.

Hannah

Deciding on the correct response to a situation

hurting her in some way. Let the children use the puppets to enact their initial response or reactions. After they have completed their story, praise some aspect of their production and then ask them to consider whether hurting the cat was the best way of dealing with the situation and if they could think of another way. Let them talk about this problem amongst themselves, and then show you their alternative solution.

If the children have developed an approach that does not involve aggression, praise them and explain why you think that this is a much better response. Compare the two reactions. The children may think of even more ways of handling the situation. Talk about these, and elicit from the children that assertive, non-aggressive responses are a better way.

Following this activity, the children draw a summary of the possible solutions. They cut out two strips of bright red paper which are then stuck across the aggressive solution, to indicate that this is not the chosen response (see photograph above).

A photographic record
For younger or less able children, use a still camera. Ask the children to re-enact their puppet play. At certain times, ask them to freeze the action and then take a photograph of the puppets. When the photographs are developed, show them to the children and let them describe what is happening in the shot. The children's description becomes the caption for the photograph. Ask the children to sort the photographs into the correct sequence and then stick them into a book or on to a piece of paper.

The naughty cat
by
Jon
Abe
Anne

The cat tripped the mouse.

The mouse was sad.

Visitors to the classroom

Many teachers encourage visitors to their classroom. These people may be valuable ancillary helpers, parent volunteers or other guests who are helping in some way in the classroom. Introducing visitors to the classroom can have a powerful effect on the atmosphere of the classroom. It is important that all adults and children who join the class, for whatever length of time, are made aware of the classroom conventions and ethos which you have worked so hard to establish.

If you and the children have determined a set of simple positive classroom rules, ensure that visitors have access to these. This will reduce the opportunities for others to unwittingly direct children in ways which you would not wish. Displaying the rules on the walls is an obvious way of advertising them, or producing a book which is made available to all visitors. The way in which you and the children interact will also give very positive messages about the approach and atmosphere in the class.

Supply, or relief, teachers will have a far easier time taking over a class if they go to a well-organised classroom in which children follow clearly described routines and codes of behaviour, and where access and availability of resources is straightforward. Producing a simple set of guidelines and advice for supply teachers is a valuable exercise.

Visitors to the classroom provide opportunities to teach children ways in which they can greet people, make them feel welcome, and show that they appreciate their help.

Involving the children

Talk to the children about ways in which people greet others. Discuss with the children what kinds of things visitors need to know - where to hang their coats, where the toilets and staffroom are, for example. When you have a visitor, ask a child or pair of children to fulfil these duties.

Bring to the class examples of Visitors' Books. Describe how they are used, and the types of information recorded in the books - names, addresses and possibly a Comments section. Get the children to design a Visitors' Book for the class, including sections that they feel would be particularly interesting for their class.

Take photographs of regular visitors to the class and display these on the wall. Ask the children why these people visit the class and get them to write simple captions for each photograph.

Developing Social Skills

Use certain selected visitors to develop the children's more general social skills. Talk to the visitor to ensure that he/she does not mind being cross-examined. Children often ask questions that more socially sensitive adults balk at! Ask the visitor to try to develop a dialogue with the children, answering the children's questions but also asking the children relevant questions about themselves. Organise a small group of children to go with the visitor and instruct them to find out as much as possible about the person in a given time, say five minutes.

If you have visitors that help, it is important that the children are aware of the contribution these people make, and that it is desirable to thank people who help.

In a class discussion, talk about saying 'thank you', and ask the children to think of occasions when they say this. Allow the children to draw pictures of their examples. In the discussion try to draw from the children when they think it is important.

I say thank you when someone gives me a present.

I say thank you when Mum makes my tea.

Showing appreciation

This activity can be used to heighten children's awareness of other languages. Tell them that you say thank you in different ways in different languages. Set them the task of trying to find out as many different ways of saying 'thank you' as possible. They can ask their families, friends, other teachers, or use information books. Collect all the examples that the children find. Get them to write or copy their words, symbols, phrases on to paper. Provide them with suitable reference books to find the flags of the appropriate countries. Cut out flat-shaped pieces of paper which the children colour appropriately and stick under their version of 'thank you'. Include the sign version of 'thank you', either by using a photograph or drawing. Display these words and flags on the wall. (See photograph on page 61.)

Thanking guests and helpers
At certain times of the year or term it may be appropriate to say a special thank you to helpers and guests to the class.

Discuss with the children how they could achieve this. If they suggest making 'thank you' cards, talk with them about how they could make it particularly personal, including things that that person likes or is interested in, or portraying events that have happened in the class.

If a present is suggested, discuss what that present should be. Again, emphasise the personal element of presents and how the person will probably appreciate a present that has involved effort or thought on the part of the donor. Encourage the children to make something for the visitor, a model or a special picture, or something that has been sewn, or a plant grown by the children.

Talk about how people wrap presents to make them look attractive and exciting. Bring in examples of different wrapping papers. Ask the children to design their own wrapping paper, thinking about the event that the gift is to commemorate. They make their designs on smaller pieces of paper and then, after discussion, a group could decide which design they think is most appropriate, and the correct size of paper is then cut. This exercise involves the important skill of estimating size. Let the children wrap the present - they may then wish to add further embellishments. Make sure that the children whose designs are not chosen know that their work is valued, by displaying all the designs.

Extend this activity with the children by asking them to think about all the other occasions when people exchange presents. Make a list with the children. Talk about the significance of these occasions or celebrations for different people, and why presents are given. Construct a display of these events. The children may be able to supply relevant photographs of family events - christenings, Bar Mitzvahs, Diwali, birthday parties, first communions, etc. Supplement the display with children's drawings and paintings and posters that you may have.

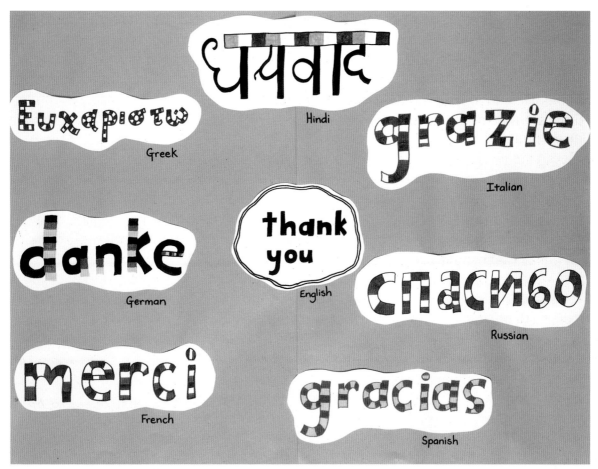

'Thank you' - an international collection

Ask the children to write or draw the kinds of presents that are exchanged on the different occasions. Discuss the rationale behind some of the gifts. Be sensitive to any children in the class who for various reasons may not celebrate certain events or rites of passage.

A thank you party

The children will note that many of these occasions are marked by parties or celebrations. When you are discussing ways in which you can thank the helpers in the class, suggest that you and the children give a 'thank you' party for the volunteers.

Involve the children with as much of the planning and organisation for the party as possible. Start with the guest list. Ask the children to decide who they think should be asked. This will include those who have made a particular contribution to the life of the class, but the children might wish to invite others. Decide when the party is to be, and where it is to be held. The children may have to check that certain rooms are free at that time.

Making invitations

Talk about the invitations and what information will need to be included. Either ask all the children to design an invitation for use with all the guests, or let individual children decide who they wish to invite, and write that particular invitation. If you choose the former method, restrict the children to black and white so that the resulting invitation is easy to photocopy. (See photograph on facing page.)

Ask the people invited to the party to reply to the invitations. Choose a group of children to collect all the replies and to make a list of all the people who have accepted. You may use a simple data base for the children to collate the acceptances.

Planning the party

As the day of the party approaches, collate with the children a list of all the things that need to be done in preparation. Plan the refreshments. If you have decided to have food, involve the children in making this. Talk about how the food will be displayed and whether there is a need for table decorations. Ask the children to design plate mats for the dishes of food, or to make paper doilies. Cut out circles of lightweight paper (or tissue paper). The children fold the circles into quarters or eighths and then cut out small shapes. When the circles are unfolded they will have patterns of holes. To strengthen the doilies, stick them on to same-sized circles of stronger, different-coloured paper.

Let the children think of ways in which they can decorate the room, and whether they think there should be background music.

Discuss with the children whether there should be any games or activities at the party. Make a list of all the possible games that could be played. Let the children decide which games would be most suitable. Having made this decision, there may be certain preparations necessary, for example, wrapping the parcel for 'Pass the Parcel', etc. Involve the children as much as possible in these preparations. Give small groups of children the responsibility for organising each game. They will have to make sure that all the equipment is ready, explain the rules to the assembled guests and ensure the smooth running of the game.

On the day of the party, allocate a child to each of the guests. Explain that it will be their job to make sure that the guests' needs are catered for, that they have enough food and drink, that they know where to put their coats, etc.

Other opportunities to welcome visitors

There will be opportunities for the children, or groups of children, to ask other groups to the class and to act as hosts. These events need not be on such a large scale but still provide valuable experiences for the children to take responsibility for others. The children may wish to invite children from other classes for a specific reason (to show them a piece of work, to share in a story) or to ask members of their family, or members of the school staff. Impress upon the children the ways in which they can make the visit a success.

Consider the wider community and ways in which the class can contribute to the life of the community. There may be groups of older people in the vicinity who would appreciate an invitation to the school to be entertained. Again, involve the children in planning the event. If they plan a concert, get them to prepare the programmes, suitably decorated, and to look after the audience as they arrive.

Investigate the possibility of the class visiting the older people in their homes to present their entertainment.

> Our Concert
> 1. One man went to mow.
> 2. Sizzling sausages
> 3. Bananas in pyjamas.

Bullying

Even in the most disciplined and positive schools there may be isolated incidents of bullying. This can take many forms. It may be overt physical intimidation, verbal abuse, or subtle and insidious exclusion from the peer group. It is vital that the children are aware that all forms of bullying are totally unacceptable within the class and the school. Developing a positive ethos in the class, and emphasising the forms of behaviour that you wish to promote, will significantly reduce the possible incidence of bullying, but there may be rare examples. You should always be very vigilant and take all incidents seriously. Training children in how to behave assertively will help them to deal with potential bullies. There are a number of powerful techniques in the assertive behaviour repertoire.

To be assertive it is necessary to state clearly what you want, using an 'I' statement. Use drama sessions to allow the children to practise this. Group the children in pairs and set up a situation where, for example, a child is pushing another. Model the possible response for the 'victim': 'Stop pushing me, Stacey. I don't like it.' Let the children swap roles and then change the situation.

After the role play, ask the children to draw the situations, with speech bubbles coming from the characters' mouths. Ask the children to fill in the speech bubbles with appropriate responses.

When a child is saying unkind things to another child, there are various options for the abused. Firstly, they could walk away. This may take practice, and the children need to think where they will go, and who they will see, having walked away. Use drama sessions to develop this skill.

Another technique is 'positive self-talk'. As the abuser says the offensive things, the abused rehearses, sub-vocally, a number of positive things about himself/herself. People are naturally reticent about saying positive things about themselves, and so it is necessary to introduce the children to this concept in steps and, possibly, in small groups as some children might be inhibited by working in larger groups.

Cut out face shapes and draw on large smiles. Talk to the children about what you consider to be your talents. Don't be shy! It could include sporting achievements, skills you have, etc. Now encourage the children to think about qualities or skills that they have.

You may find that the children will suggest things about other children. Then write or draw these attributes in the smile on the face. These may be displayed, or it might be more appropriate for the children to keep them privately.

With this preparation, the children will now have a script for the positive self-talk. If they are unable to walk away from someone who is verbally abusing them, or their family, they block out the words by repeating good things about themselves. This should be done sub-vocally, but some children will need to practise it out loud to start with. Praise the children's efforts.

For older children, 'fogging' is another way of coping with abuse. This involves taking the sting out of any critical statement by neutralising it. For example, if the bully says 'You smell', the victim can reply 'Maybe I do', or if the attack is 'Your Mum has horrible hair', the response could be 'You might think so.' This is a sophisticated technique, and should only be used with children with an appropriate level of confidence.

Certain techniques can be further enhanced by using the 'broken record' method. If someone is trying to upset you, repeat a chosen response over and over again - this is very frustrating for the aggressor, and quickly wears them down. Demonstrate the method and allow the children the chance to practise it. Explain why this is called the broken record method: some children may be unfamiliar with records, and you may have to rename it the 'broken tape'. Cut out circles and ask the children to choose a phrase that they feel would be useful to use. Ask them to write this phrase round the circle several times to reinforce the technique.

Having provided the children with a repertoire of approaches to someone who is bullying them, bring all this work together. Describe a possible situation where someone is being unkind to them. Ask them to think about what they would do, and to illustrate their responses. Discuss the various suggestions with all the children, and then display them on the class wall.

Someone is saying nasty things...

I'd walk away

I wouldn't listen

I'd tell them to stop

If a child chooses to tell an adult that someone is being unkind to them, it is very important that their complaint is taken seriously and they know that it will be followed up. Such situations require careful professional judgement as you do not want to encourage unjustified tale-telling, but children need to know that adults will do everything to preserve their safety and rights.

Dealing with bullies

Bullies need to know clearly that their behaviour is not acceptable. Sanctions and consequences of their behaviour need to be enforced. It is important, however, that the adult does not model bullying type behaviour when dealing with the miscreants. It is to be hoped that as well as showing displeasure, the teachers and adults involved can work with the bullies to provide them with alternative ways of behaving. Such an approach takes time, but it is time well spent.

If a child has been found to be bullying, you need to lead them to ways in which they can exert their power or control for the good, and not to the detriment, of others.

Find a quiet time with the child who is bullying. This is time when you are working with them and not punishing them. Explain that you are with them because you think that they have been giving someone a bad time. This should be said calmly and not accusingly. The child may deny it, but this is your time to use the broken record technique, quietly repeating that you feel that there is someone who is not very happy because of the child's behaviour. Once the child has shown a glimmer of agreement, ask them what they think they could do to make the other child's time in school happier. Listen to the suggestions and talk about them, praising the ideas and showing your obvious pleasure that the child is thinking of positive approaches.

Provide the child with a piece of paper and ask him/her to draw ideas for improving the lot of others. Say that you are going to keep this drawing safely and that you will be watching the child's behaviour to see if you can 'catch' him/her doing any of these good things.

It is vital that you keep your word and if you see the child behaving positively towards others, to show your extreme pleasure. Some children will respond best to public praise, whereas others may welcome a private, previously agreed, sign of pleasure, for example a 'thumbs up'.

Helping individual children to manage their own behaviour

Children recording their own behaviour

There are some children who somehow encourage bullies. They may, subconsciously, respond to the attention that being bullied gives them. Sensitive work is required with these children to enable them to develop skills to allow them to interact with their peers positively and to gain attention from purposeful interactions and relationships. It may be necessary to model certain behaviour with the children and to structure their play with non-threatening peers to demonstrate alternative ways of interacting.

The ultimate goal of any behaviour management structure is for the children **to manage their own behaviour.** No matter how good your overall structure is, there may be on occasions individual children who do not respond and who are being troublesome by interfering with the work of others, shouting out, wandering around the classroom. For the few children who are a constant source of this low level disruptive behaviour, it is necessary to plan individual behaviour management programmes and for these to be in a form readily understood and 'owned' by the child.

There are many forms of behaviour management programmes, and a description of a number of them follow. It is important to understand that no matter what programme you use, there are a number of principles which must be adhered to if the programme is to succeed.

- Behaviour management programmes are about rewarding positive/good behaviour, NOT punishing bad behaviour. Rewarding good behaviour reinforces the behaviour and raises the child's self-esteem. Punishing bad behaviour reduces self-esteem and the child gains all-important attention for the wrong reasons.
- It must be explained to the child exactly what the behaviour is that you wish to improve.
- Explain exactly the method you are going to use.
- If the class is taken by other teachers or you have a classroom helper, ensure that they understand exactly what you are trying to do. Their co-operation is essential if you are to obtain consistency and success.

Gathering evidence

Before starting any form of behaviour management programme, it is important to have gathered evidence of the unacceptable behaviour and to have ensured that all the children understand that the behaviour is unacceptable. To use the previous example: it would be unrealistic to expect children not to shout out if it has not been explained to them exactly what you expect when asking questions, or they are asking for help. Give a clear explanation to the whole class.

Having established your expectations with the class, these can be reinforced with simple illustrations which are displayed under the heading of 'Good Classroom Behaviour'. You can now observe the children.

Design a simple 'tick chart' for your own use to record how often the child does not conform to the expected behaviour.

Name		Week		
M	✓✓✓	✓	✓✓✓	✓✓
T	✓✓	✓✓	✓✓	
W		✓✓✓✓	✓	✓
T	✓✓✓	✓✓✓		✓
F	✓✓		✓✓✓	✓✓

At the end of each session, or sooner if possible, put a tick on the chart every time the child does **not** achieve what you expect. Ask other teachers to do the same. Keep this record for at least two weeks. At the end of this period you will have evidence of how often the child did not manage the expected behaviour, and if there are any sessions or times of the week that they find particularly difficult.

Planning the Behaviour Management Programme

You are now ready to consider modifying the behaviour. You need to be REALISTIC. Set a target for the first week. Using the 'calling out' example, look for a twenty percent reduction in the number of times the child calls out. With praise and consistency you should see a 80/90% reduction within a matter of weeks. Do not look for perfection - but more what is acceptable and manageable in the classroom.

Plan for the end of the programme!

Decide how long you are going to use it for. An endless programme becomes self-defeating. Plan for a maximum of six weeks, with a review after three to see what progress is being made and if there are any modifications necessasry.

Involve parents

They need to know what you are doing, and why you are doing it. Enlist their help in reinforcing the good behaviour.

Setting up and running the programme

INVOLVE THE CHILD. The golden rule for all behaviour modification is to involve the child to gain joint ownership.

Progress Charts

A very simple but effective way of behaviour is to use a progress chart. Draw up a chart on A4 paper as illustrated.

Name _____					Week _____
					Comments
M					
T					
W					
T					
F					

Often a simple star system is used. Explain to the child that she will be given a gold star at the end of each session if she has not shouted out. She can then stick her star on to her chart. Give the child the exact time when you will be starting the programme. For example, discuss the chart on Friday to start on Monday.

Contact the parents explaining the programme is about to start, and that their daughter will be bringing home the recording sheet each evening, and that they should praise the child for every star on the chart.
It is vital that the child has ownership of the programme and therefore the chart should remain with the child, not you.

Hand the sheet to the child on Monday morning, with a positive comment about how you are looking forward to seeing lots of stars on the chart at the end of the day. At the end of each session, if the child has succeeded, praise her and hand out the star for her to stick on the chart in the relevant place. If the child did not succeed,

Name _____					Week _____
					Comments
M	✳	✳	✳	✳	
T	✳	✳	✳		
W	✳	✳	✳	✳	Great!
T		✳		✳	
F	✳	✳	✳	✳	fantastic

explain exactly why she did not receive a star, and say how you are looking forward to her managing to achieve a star for the next lesson, thus avoiding criticism.

The time interval is crucial. Where, from the evidence gathered, it is obvious that the child cannot manage this length of time, reduce the time accordingly. The aim is to BUILD ON SUCCESS.

You may wish to give an extra reward at the end of a successful period, e.g. a whole day of stars. This could be a large plain star which the child can decorate for display on the 'Good News' board.

Iona got all her stars today – Well done.

There are endless varieties of ways in which you can use these simple progress charts. For example, if the child has an interest in cars, use a small cut-out car for a sticker, with a large one for the child to decorate at the end of the period. If the child is interested in dogs, use a cut-out dog, etc. The more interesting it is for the child, the more likely the success. Smiley faces usually go down well!

Staying on task

There are a variety of ways of assisting children to stay on task, and they can be fun for the children too! Making a game of staying on task can be enjoyable for the children, and these games can be used for individuals, groups or whole classes.

Either record a simple sound, for example a handbell on a cassette recorder, or have a handbell or rattle in the classroom with you. The sound should be made at varying intervals, from one minute to ten minute intervals.

Produce a simple recording chart.

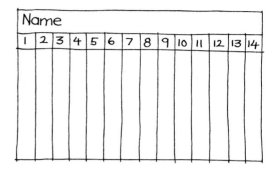

Explain to the children exactly what the game is. Children are very honest and will record accurately. A reward system using 'Smiley faces' can be used. At the end of the lesson, give out a sheet of smiley faces and allow the children to colour in one face for each tick on the chart. Again, these can be displayed on the 'Good News' board.

Contracts

Occasionally a child may not respond to a behaviour management programme. Any programme that does not achieve an improvement quickly should be abandoned to avoid building on failure. On these occasions, it may be that a contract approach would be successful.

The underlying principle is that contracts should be simply worded, illustrated, displayed and signed by all parties.

Example - Peter persists in writing or drawing on other children's work.

Stage 1 - Explain clearly and quietly to Peter, on his own, that it is not fair to write or draw on the work of other children, and that you know he would like to stop doing it. You have a very grown-up way of helping him.

Stage 2 - Show Peter the contract you have drawn up.

Stage 3 - Read through the contract and explain that he is agreeing to try and stop writing or drawing on the work of others. Talk about the illustration.

Stage 4 - Ask Peter to put his name to say that he agrees to the contract. You sign your name to show that you agree with the contract.

Stage 5 - Ask your classroom assistant to sign the contract in front of Peter.

Stage 6 - Explain to Peter that you will be telling his parents about the contract and sending it home for them to sign.

Stage 7 - Explain to Peter that you will be telling the class about the contract and how it will help him. You will also display a copy of the contract on the progress board.

Stage 8 - Contact Peter's parents to explain the contract and send it home for them to sign.

Stage 9 - Explain to the class and display the contract.

Stage 10 - At the end of each session, praise Peter when he has managed to stick to his contract and put a Smiley face on the displayed contract.

If Peter fails, refer back to the contract. Repeat what you all agreed and say how you are looking forward to giving him a smiley face at the end of the next session.

For details of further Belair Publications please write to:
BELAIR PUBLICATIONS LTD.
P.O. Box 12, Twickenham TW1 2QL, England.

For sales and distribution (outside USA and Canada):
FOLENS PUBLISHERS, Albert House, Apex Business Centre,
Boscombe Road, Dunstable, Beds. LU5 4RL, England.

For sales and distribution in USA and Canada:
Belair Publications USA, 116 Corporation Way, Venice, Florida, 34292.